# PIP Away and Don't Delay

# PIP Away and Don't Delay

## Personal Improvement Program

Ted Lennox

Order this book online at www.trafford.com
or email orders@trafford.com

Most Trafford titles are also available at major online book retailers.

Printed in the United States of America.

ISBN: 978-1-4907-4714-9 (sc)
ISBN: 978-1-4907-4716-3 (hc)
ISBN: 978-1-4907-4715-6 (e)

Library of Congress Control Number: 2014917001

*Trafford rev. 09/19/2014*

www.trafford.com

North America & international
toll-free: 1 888 232 4444 (USA & Canada)
fax: 812 355 4082

Personal Improvement Program

Written by Ted Lennox

This book is written and is only loaded with suggestions that might be of some help or interest to some people. It is in no way meant to tell anyone what to do or what to think or how to live. It is meant to encourage you, the reader, to think for yourself and to follow your own life's path. In fact, that is exactly what I hope this book will do for me. Encourage me to follow that path of life that God wants me to pursue.

Now, and this is important. If you are kind enough to read the book, and if you have any suggestions, ideas, thoughts, or questions, I would encourage you to contact me for a discussion.

Here is my contact information.

Home telephone number: clearly understandable. 313 846:0318

(I'm tempted to tell you that the last two numbers are my age, but since I want to be honest throughout this book I'll tell you the truth. My age is exactly the reverse of the last two numbers in my phone number.

Cell Phone Number: 734 787:3508
Please don't do what I did! That is I called my daughter Amy, at twelve o'clock one night. I'll treat you the same way she treated me!!!!

My email address is tedlennox@gmail.com

My home address is: Ted Lennox 15081 Ford Road, PT 419 (PT stands for Parkview terrace.)

Dearborn, Michigan 48126

If you read this book, keep it fun and thoughtful.

Do your own thinking and follow your own path as you go through your exciting life.

As I read this introduction, I realize that we, you and I, are on a similar path. That is, I have not completed my journey of learning, living, and growing. I will and I need to be Pipping from birth to death. Keep in mind that PIP stands for Personal Improvement Program. Moreover, I hope to commit myself to literally enjoying the trail.

Note: I said Trail not Trial. please tolerate my attempt at fun.)

So what I am stating is that we are all on a road in life. So forward we go, into this exciting adventure we will call life.

# Contents

# Chapter 1

# Introduction To Pip

You might be asking "What is PIP?"
This chapter will give an introduction to Pip!
So go ahead and read away!
But whatever you do, enjoy this day!

?????????--

As you already know, our culture, in fact, our world is filled with acronyms. Some are so common that we all almost think of them as words. Here are just a few examples. We just say or write the IRS. I'm so use to that acronym that I had to stop and think just now what IRS stands for. It, as we know, is an acronym for Internal Revenue Service.

I think we just use the letters FBI. That, of course, means Federal Bureau of investigation. Permit me one more. CEO means Chief Executive Officer. The CEO of a company is the head or the leader of the company. You've got me going with these acronyms. I'd kind of enjoy seeing how many of them I could state, but for your sake, my reader, I will stop here. I challenge you to go ahead and think of five more. I'm going to do the same right now.

I have for fun titled this book PIP. PIP is an acronym standing for:

Personal Improvement Program.

The major idea or theme in this book is that we are all on a journey through life. My suggestions in the chapters that follow are that we all keep PIPPING. In other words, I am recommending that we keep Personally Improving. That is, from birth until death we might want to keep learning, improving, and growing, if I can use the word growing meaningfully!

Now, then, permit me to be very clear. This book, in no way, is meant to tell you what to do or how to live. In fact, it is meant to encourage you to follow your own path through life. In other words to keep PIPPING from birth until death. Thus, have your own Personal Improvement Program. So that's my friendly recommendation to myself and to others. That is, keep Pipping throughout life.

The chapters that follow are just my thoughts and suggestions. Please do your own thinking, and follow your own life's path. I will be doing the same thing.

Often as we travel through our lives others tell us what to do. Sometimes we find their suggestions to be helpful and meaningful. If so we should be comfortable following their advice.

Then there will be times that what others wish you to do you do not agree with them. In those cases you should follow your own direction. That direction being yours internally.

Now there certainly could be circumstances where advice from the outside would be better to follow, so you should follow it. But note: you have made the internal decision to follow whatever it is that you think is a good idea. So you are using internal guidance even in cases like I just mentioned.

Let me reiterate, (hey! there's a word I seldom use,) practice doing your own thinking. Then, follow that thinking of yours. Be free to learn from your thinking and from your actions. Thus, based on your thinking and learning go right ahead and keep improving.

I must be very clear before terminating this exciting chapter. What is coming in this book will be thirteen more chapters.

Those chapters are simply suggestions and ideas for you to think over. I am not, once again, I am not telling you what to think or what to do. You should decide that based on your own life.

Chapter Summary

This book is titled PIP. That means Personal Improvement Program. The word Personal is mighty important. It means you should be in charge of your life, your thinking, and behaving. The outside world should not control you. So trust yourself, do your own thinking, have confidence in your thinking. We've gotten off to a good start, so I will proceed to chapter two, namely Enjoy Every Moment.

As I said at the opening of this chapter called PIP, I hope to start each chapter with a poem that sums up what the main theme of the chapter will be. That's something I enjoy about poetry. You can say so much in so few words. Now the danger in saying so much in a few words is that one could get misinterpreted. First, I hope my poems do not get misinterpreted, and second I hope that the chapter following the poem will clarify everything and add to the chapter.

So we'll start each chapter with a poem. Because one absolutely wonderful gift God has given us, is the ability to laugh, each chapter shall end with a riddle or with a joke. They are to encourage laughing, and laughter tends to help us all function more positively and effectively. One additional guideline when it comes to being humorous! Every joke in this book will be uplifting and positive. There are jokes out there that I strongly am against. Those are jokes that downgrade people. For instance, there are jokes about blonde ladies that indicate they lack intelligence. First, that is hogwash, blonde ladies are intelligent. Second there are jokes about different cultures, polish people for instance. They indicate that Polish people aren't too smart. First, Polish people are smart; second, our humor should definitely elevate people and let them know they are intelligent. We'll get to more of that in a later chapter.

Chapter Humor

Chapter Homework!
Each evening before you go to bed I would like you to eat a
spoonful of shoe polish and a bite of yeast.

You may be wondering why I would make such an assignment!!!

Well, here's the answer. If you have a spoon of shoe polish and
a bite of yeast before going to bed, in the morning you will
"rise and Shine". I dare you to try it!

# Chapter 2

# Enjoy Each Moment

ENJOY THE MOMENT

Enjoy the moment if you will,
Happiness your heart each moment should fill.
Keep God with you all the way,
Keep Him with you night and day!

In a sense each moment is a gift,
So use each moment your life to lift,
Fill each moment with joy and zest,
That will help you to do your best!

So off I go to follow my advice,
To myself and to others I'll try to be nice!
So here is what I am now confessing,
I'll try my best to make each moment a blessing!
?????????--

The main idea that I hope to discuss in this chapter is that we might make a commitment to enjoy each moment of our life. As I think about the above statement, I am aware that life does have its ups and downs. There are times filled with joy and other times that might be sad or disheartening. However, I guess what I am trying to say in terms of Enjoying Life is that we should focus our minds and feelings on enjoying the moment. That's something that I shall practice doing. Again, that is, to enjoy whatever and whereever we are at during any given time. Thus, while eating dinner, talking with a friend, waiting for a bus on a cold winter day, it is still possible to focus on the joy of the moment.

Five years and eight months ago my wonderful wife Laura left for Heaven. Shortly after that my daughter Amy read me a book called something like:

The Present Is Your Present.

The thought in the book was that we have been given a present, that present is the present. The notion in the book is that we should take that present, again the present, and make the most of it. Thus, enjoy your present, think of it as a present. What a powerful concept!
I will call Amy today and find out the name and author of the book.

There is my suggestion for this chapter. Maybe you'll find it of some value. I shall focus my being on enjoying the moment.

What is being suggested in this chapter is the idea that we might make life Fun. If we are concentrating on enjoying the moment, then life here on this planet for us cannot help but be fun. So if we are out taking a walk, watching television, doing the washing, if we think about it we can have fun. If I were young again and in say fifth grade, I would put forth an effort to have a good time in every class. What exciting fun it could have been to learn the multiplication tables, to find out about the countries in this great world, or learn about nouns and verbs.

Do You Remember Me

Perhaps this is a strange way to tell you one of the most wonderful Enjoy The Moment stories of my life, but I shall tell it to you. I personally find stories that are touching, personal, or perhaps romantic fascinating and thrilling. So here I go!

On Memorial Day in 1954 I was a junior at Michigan State University. A student group from People's Church spent the weekend canoeing down the Au Sabo River up north in Michigan. I and my girlfriend went together for the adventure. It turned out to be an adventure! It ended our relationship. At the time I was so sad and hurting.

Upon getting back to East Lansing, I went in the living room in the College House which was connected to the church. At the table was an 18 year old freshman girl. We had a pleasant and friendly talk for probably fifteen or twenty minutes. Her name was Laura, by the way.

Now jumping forward six years with this story to June of 1960. I was attending summer school pursuing my teaching certificate. I was quietly sitting in the Union cafeteria by myself eating lunch. All of a sudden sort of out of nowhere there was a young lady standing to my immediate right.

She pleasantly said, "Do you remember me?" I said something like, "I'd better, since you remember me!" After a little discussion I did remember her.

Those four words "do you remember me?" started a whole new adventure for us both. That adventure lasted 47 years and 11 months.

Permit me to return to the purpose of this wonderful story. What seemed back on Memorial Day in 1954 to be a really sad occurrence in my life led to the greatest friendship, love, and marriage I could have had. I personally believe that God had Laura waiting their for me.

The bottom line of this story and the main idea of this chapter is the notion that WHATEVER OCCURS IN One's LIFE interpret as being something for the good. Construe it with such an outlook that you view it as opening the door to real good things. Let me reiterate, there's a word I seldom use, so reiterating regardless of what is occurring in one's life be sure to enjoy it internally. Make the best of it and keep joy in your heart.

Summary

My suggestion in this chapter is simple, but so, so important at least to me. It is:

Enjoy each and every moment. Think of the present as a present from God!

Chapter Humor:

Question: Why did the turkey cross the road twice?

Answer: To show that he wasn't a chicken!

# Chapter 3
# Be Self-Confident

Be Confident

In order to function as I should,
To myself I must be good.
I must be confident with my every thought,
This is wisdom that I should have been taught!

Confidence is a great attribute,
To a wholesome life it's truly the route.
I must be confident with my every feeling.
When it comes to confidence, there's no wheeling, no dealing!

?????????-

This chapter will have two main topics. First, we will consider
what I mean by self-confidence. Then, we will explore some ways
or techniques for developing self-confidence. I think that this
chapter and the last chapter on enjoying the moment, for me, are
the two most important chapters in this book. If we can make it
a habit to ENJOY EVERY MOMENT, and to be CONFIDENT one's life
will move forward in a happy way. Please note that the words
ENJOY and CONFIDENT are in capital letters. Moreover, enjoying
the moment and being confident will permit us and allow us to
function at our best. That is, to live with joy and to use our
God given abilities to their fullest extent.

I just read the above and I am aware that I originally mistitled
the Chapter. At first I titled it Be Confident. I just went to
the top of this chapter and renamed it. The new title is BE
SELF-CONFIDENT. Thus I have added the word Self. What I am
inferring in the chapter title is that we should develop our own

confidence. That is, our confidence should be internally developed and not dependent upon external development.

I must be careful to be clear, we certainly can learn from outside sources, but we should personally decide what is right or what is best for us individually. Again, we should think for ourselves and not allow others to think for us, or control us. Our thinking and controlling should be internal not external.

This chapter has been written now of quite some time, but I have decided to add this, what I think, is an important paragraph. Throughout my life I have been trying to find the path to happiness, fulfillment, and confidence. At Michigan State I took classes in philosophy, effective living, psychology, and so forth. I was seeking the answers to being happy, joyful, and confident. I guess my as sumption being that the answers come from the outside. If I were to teach such a class, my aim and my goal would to be to help and to encourage each student to:

First, be happy, confident, and comfortable where they are, at any given time.

Second, keep growing and learning and finding fulfillment and joy in your life as it is at THIS MOMENT.

Third: Keep life enjoyable, exciting, peaceful, and adventurous.

Fourth: Do your own thinking and trust yourself, be confident.

Now, what do I mean by self-confidence. I could go to the dictionary and look it up, or I could check what other authors have to say. I may do that also, but for now I want to tell you what I am trying to convey when I say we all should develop self-confidence. Please wish me well.

Here's what I am expressing when I talk about Self-confidence.

1. We should be our own guide. We should think for ourselves and believe and trust our own thinking. What an exciting way to live!

2. Thus, the outside world should not be in charge or control of our thinking about ourselves.

3. Right from the beginning we should be taught and we should learn to follow our own unique path in life.

So! do your own thinking and feeling. Trust and believe in yourself. Be your own guide. In other words, be internally directed. Do your own thinking. Believe in yourself.

Now it is on to the second part of this chapter. That is, ideas and techniques for developing and building confidence in yourself. What follows will be suggestions that may be helpful. You may have additional ideas and thoughts for building self-confidence. Use all and any techniques that you find helpful and of value. Remember, keep having fun and enjoying each moment.

Ideas And Techniques For Being Self-confident

My first suggestion and it is basic or fundamental. Any other ideas that I may mention will be built on this single suggestion. So! get ready, here it comes!

Watch with great care what you say to yourself. Say and think to yourself words that are positive and confidence building. Build confident, joyful, and happy words into your internal thinking. Think words that are confidence building. Eliminate any negative words that you say to yourself or to others about yourself. Perhaps you will allow me to write some positive statement that hopefully will lead to our being confident and peaceful. Please just think about what follows, and then perhaps use them in your thinking, or use similar thoughts that work better for you.

1. I am a confident person.
2. I am capable.
3. I can do what I decide to do.
4. I am proud of what I do all through the day.
5. I focus my mind on enjoying each moment.
6. I enjoy myself.
7. I enjoy being with others.
8. I keep God with me constantly.

Now, let me talk with you about the last statement. In terms of God being with me constantly, that has been a journey for me. I'd like to explain all that to you, my reader, but the emphasis in this chapter is on building confidence. Maybe I'll conclude this book with a chapter about God's importance in my life and the complex trail I followed in the development of opening my heart to God. Let me just say at this point, God has guided me throughout my life and I am so grateful. As I've digressed to talk about God and my friendship with him-her I have decided to end this book with a chapter telling you about how important God has been in my life even when I was not aware of God's presence and guidance.

Permit me to digress for a moment. (There's a word I like to use, but seldom get a chance, the word digress!)

Second, focus your thinking and your feeling on the right now. Live in the present. Enjoy the present. This does not mean that you won't look backward or forward, it emphasizes being in the now. Let the past have a positive influence on your present and your future. In terms of the past evaluate things that took place and enjoy the positive experiences. As for the negative or the experiences that put limits on you, override them and change your outlook so they help you do better right now and in the future.

Back six years ago my wonderful wife Laura passed away. My daughters and I went through a great deal of difficulty as we missed her ever so much. My daughter Amy read me a book called something like the present is a present. That book said so much. I will talk with Amy and get the exact name of the book. It might be of interest to some of you.

Personally, I do look at my past. If I could go back and do things differently I would, but most importantly, the past is a life trail that I am on. I try to make that trail better and more exciting and meaningful as I go.

Thirdly, load your mind with words and pictures that are positive and loaded with happiness and fun. So monitor continually your thoughts and your feelings. Find the good in every experience, and build your immediate and distant future on good thinking and picturing in the present.

Before concluding this chapter I have an urge to share a personal story with all of you. It is a life story about Iggy Conrad and Fendley Collins. Please do not loose sight of the notion that they were both highly important in my life, and I thank God for both of them.

Let's look at Iggy Conrad first. Iggy was the wrestling coach at Sexton High when I was a student. I also would consider him a friend. Iggy helped me to be what I think of as an average wrestler.

We were all trained to be physically fit and to know and do our various wrestling maneuvers. That was good. Now, what never was approached in any way was our thinking about our ability and potential.

If I were a wrestling coach today, my team and I would take time during EVERY practice to evaluate, to modify, and to focus on how capable and able we are. In other words, we'd learn to believe in our wonderful abilities that God has provided. In other words, positive, constructive, and joyful thinking would be an integral part of our training sessions. I would teach the word-for-word vocabulary that leads to happiness, confidence, and internal success.

What I have said above about my wonderful high school coach also applies directly to my fabulous Findley Collins my college coach. Bottom thought in all areas of life we need to think positively, we need to think confidently, and we should enjoy Every that's Every Moment!!!!

SUMMARY:

1. Develop your self-confidence!
2. The key to self-confidence is what you say to yourself.
3. Say positive, happy, enjoyable words to yourself!
4. Avoid and eliminate negative words and thoughts about yourself.
5. Focus on using PIP throughout your day, that is, keep paying attention to your own Personal Improvement Program.

Chapter Joke:

My grand daughter asked me this one a few days ago.

Grandpa: Why did the cookie go to the doctor?

Answer: Because it was feeling Crummy!

Please bear with me as I include another poem that expresses the vital importance of confidence!

CONFIDENCE

I live each moment in a confident way,
From this commitment I shall never sway;
I believe that God put me here on earth,
He meant me to live fully right from my birth!

So forward I go with a confident mind,
To myself and to others I will always be kind!
Each thought will be a confident thought,
This from birth I should have been taught!

Starting right now I will truly think,
Positive words that will not let me sink!
With the words that I shall use I cannot fail,
From this moment on I surely will sail!

# Chapter 4
# We Are All Intelligent

The title of the following poem is about You, the person reading the poem. So please keep in mind that you are reading about yourself. Now to the poem.

I Am Intelligent

I am confident that I am intelligent,
It has always been here and it never shall went!
My mind is sharp, and always alert,
I use my intelligence to live and never to hurt!

I keep my mind buoyant and Sharp,
I try to feel like I'm playing a harp!
I am intelligent wherever I go!
My mind is fast it's not slow!

I note that you are intelligent too,
Intelligence is not reserved just for a few,
Each one of us has a terrific mind,
Look around and that's what you'll find!

Use your intelligence to pursue the good,
To do that is something that we all should!
We all have such a wonderful mind,
Use it to live and to be kind!

?????????--

Let me open this chapter with an important statement especially in this world in which we all reside. That statement being that you are intelligent. We all need to build that kind of outlook and belief into our conscious and subconscious minds. Let me repeat the thought both for you and for me. We are all intelligent. When you believe the statement, WE ARE ALL INTELLIGENT, we function better and more effectively. Further, we are happier because of our knowing that we are intelligent. What we believe about ourselves is so important. Our beliefs should make us limitless. We should not place limits on our thinking and feeling about ourselves. As we grow up, our parents and our teachers should focus on helping us to believe in ourselves. Our parents and our teachers should have the goal of helping us to build positive beliefs about ourselves. We should learn to respect ourselves and to respect one another. We need to learn to dream and to set goals. However, the most important thing is that we believe that we are capable and able human beings.

At first I thought of starting this chapter talking about the IQ myth and how it can limit us. However, I decided to start with the uplifting and positive notion that we are INTELLIGENT and that we should not set Limitations on ourselves. Maybe I might add that we should learn not to let others put limits on our lives. In fact, others should help and encourage us with the beliefs that we are able, capable, and unlimited. We all should do that with one another.

Now so that I do not get misinterpreted let me carry this a little further and explain what I mean. That is what do I mean by believing that we are unlimited. I don't mean that you can go outside and wave your arms and fly to the moon. But let's say you are a runner. Let's say you now run a mile in 13 minutes. You might think, hey! I can run faster. I will set a goal of running a twelve minute mile. Then as you work toward this goal and say in a short time you accomplish a twelve minute mile, then, you might set a goal of running an eleven minute mile.

Remember, the concept in this chapter is to believe in yourself and not to set limits or barriers for yourself in your thinking. Instead view yourself as unlimited and pursue the goals you set for yourself. The bottom line in this chapter is that you are INTELLIGENT.

Perhaps I have strayed from the main theme of this chapter, so let me express it again. The theme is that you are intelligent. You are capable. You are a competent human being. So what is the theme or major concept in this chapter? It is that you are intelligent! And to be honest I do apply this to myself and to you. You are Intelligent and so am I.

One of the tragedies in schools today is that we measure children's intelligence. We give youngsters what we call an IQ score. IQ stands for intelligence quotient. For example, it is recorded that Sue has an IQ of 108, or Tom's IQ is 106. People are given an IQ or intelligence quotient.

First off, when a psychologist measures a child's intelligence, how well that child functions depends on Many things. Let me just name a few. One thing being is the confidence level at the given time of the IQ test. Another factor is the health of the youngster at the time of the test. A third factor might be how much sleep and the quality of the sleep the child has had before the IQ test. Another item would be the flow of the blood and oxygen going to the brain while the test is being given. Another thing to consider is the relationship of the child to the IQ tester. We could add more items, and probably right now you have some factors that you would suggest effect a child or a person's functioning at any given time.

Where I am going with all this is that measuring Iq and putting people at a certain Iq score is a terrible idea. I apologize to all of you who measure IQ or believe it is a good thing. I simply believe that it might place limits on us. So my thinking is that measuring intelligence should not be done at all. Not under any circumstances. In fact, school psychologists should be fervent about inspiring and stimulating youngsters to have confidence and believe in themselves. Kids should learn to reach for the stars, to enjoy and to focus on their Abilities not their Limits.

I just read the above paragraph, and it really inspired my mind. What a great job a school psychologist could have! That job being to help youngsters to be highly self-confident, to enjoy living every moment, and to believe that they are intelligent.

Some people might say wait, measuring Intelligence Quotients is how we plan education for children. If so, that should not be done. We should just take each child or each person and determine their level of functioning in a specific area, and then start teaching them from where they are. By this I mean, let's say we are deciding what to teach in math to a specific individual. We should measure what that individual knows, and then start teaching him or her from their level of understanding.

Let's say I am learning basic math. If I am able to add and subtract nicely, then my math class should move on into multiplication and division.

In other words, I am saying that we should not limit one another. Rather, we should figure out where we are in any given area and work from there. Growth and setting no limitations should be the thinking.

What I am working at getting across is that measuring IQ should not be done. It should not be allowed. It will only set limitations in people's thinking. I personally don't think there should be anything like Iq being done to we human beings. That only sets limits on us.

May I add another notion to this idea that we are all intelligent. Often times in high schools students are rated or ranked as number one, number two, number three, or number 210 in their particular class. To me that is so sad. We should not be ranking people in a class. That should not be involved in our schools or elsewhere.

Chapter Summary

You are intelligent. We all should know this truth. So believe in your own unique special abilities. Measuring IQ's should be forbidden. The concept that we have an intelligence quotient should not be part of education, nor part of a society that aims for each of us to be unlimited. We should not place limitations on ourselves or on others.

Chapter Humor:

Question: a duck, a frog, and a skunk wanted to go to a movie. The movie cost one dollar, which one couldn't go because he couldn't afford it?

Answer: The duck could go it had a bill, the frog could go it had a greenback, but the skunk only had a scent!!!

# Chapter 5

# We Have Marvelous Memories

Good Memory

My memory is absolutely great,
I remember everything that you cannot debate!
I remember and interpret everything in a positive way,
This is true, that I do say!

Remember, remember, everything that I do say,
Construe everything in a positive way,
Let nothing you remember hold you back,
I have a positive memory, that I do not lack!

Chapter Preview

In this chapter I will be writing about our wonderful memories.
We do have the choice of making and using our memories for good
and for positive use. A person's memory can also be used to
limit and hold them from reaching for the stars if you will let
me use that phrase. By reaching for the stars I mean to keep
your mind unlimited. Again, I am saying allow yourself to dream,
set goals, and work toward those goals. As part of this process
please believe in yourself and do your own thinking.

I will be suggesting some techniques that we might use to help us
remember what we want to remember. I wish I could provide some
techniques to allow us to forget things we should not remember.
That is something I will be contemplating as I write this
chapter. For now what I am saying is that we want a good memory,
but we want our memory to focus on positive and confidence
building things. We want to learn how to use memory in a way

that helps us to live a productive and fulfilling life here on earth.

This introduction has really stimulated me to think about memory and its use for enriching one's life. So far in this book the first four chapters for me have been easy to write because I have just written and shared with you what I at least try to do daily. Again, that does not mean that I am perfect, but I do aim at Enjoying EVERY Moment, Being Self-confident, and believing that we are all intelligent. Please do not think that I am telling you about how intelligent I am. Rather, I'm saying that We are All Intelligent. We need to believe that, we need to value that, so I'm saying that You are intelligent.

As I write this, I am becoming aware that I do not have well-defined techniques for the use of our great memories. So, you have inspired and stimulated me to think about how one can improve their memory.

You are inspiring me to PIP in all areas. So please read, think, and improve on what I present. I'll do the same! I will reflect upon what follows to decide if or what can help me improve my memory.

I will first encourage us, you and me, to believe that we have a good memory, and that we can remember things. Tell yourself that you can remember things. Think positively about your ability to remember.

Second, when you find yourself becoming a little tense just take a few deep breaths. Deep breathing helps one relax and gets the blood and oxygen flowing through your system.

Take time several days a week to get some kind of physical exercise. By that I mean, take a nice walk 3 or 4 times per week. Running is real good, as is bike riding, and really anything that gets your heart pumping and blood flowing.

Focus your mind on what you are doing and on what you want to remember. Perhaps review in your mind what you want to recall. By that I mean, let's say you are reading the newspaper and you want to remember the information in the article you are reading. Perhaps review the article after you have read it. By review in this situation I mean to run through it in your mind. Or, perhaps you have just discussed something with a friend. It could be helpful to run through what you want to remember in your mind. I think I shall start to do this myself.

When your mind is rested, and you are not tired, it may be easier to remember things. Now, maybe this is just me, I tend to be sharper and my mind works more effectively if I am not too tired. That might not be true for you.

I just sent my grandson Dave, who is currently a college student an article by Steve Gillman titled 27 exam taking tips. I thought it might help him in his classes.

Another notion that I might mention is to get adequate sleep especially before you are going to take an exam. Again, this might help you to be able to use your mind better and more positively.

There are a number of Compact Discs and books that provide memory development and techniques available. Again, I should be able to include a variety of memory development skills that you might put to use, but by writing this chapter I am aware that this is an area I need to look into far more than I have.

Chapter Summary

I think that I have made my point. So let me conclude this chapter. Here is my summary.

* 1. Believe that you can remember.
* 2. Practice deep breathing and relaxing.
* 3. Concentrate on what you are doing, in other words pay

attention.
* 4. Get adequate sleep.
* 5. Use your brain, learn something, do puzzles, read, think, talk.

Chapter Humor:

Question: What did the pig say at the beach on a hot summer's day?

Answer: I'm bacon!

# Chapter 6

# Develop Your Creativity

Let me begin by thinking about what it means to be creative. One common expression we hear when creativity is being discussed is that we should "think out of the box." That is a rather neat expression, and it does encourage a person to be creative.

I will play with that notion "thinking out of the box" and see where it might lead us. It basically means thinking in a different way from the usual way of thinking. Perhaps, we might say when we are introduced to a person the "in the box" thing to do would be to say something like: "Nice to meet you", or "I'm glad to meet you." If we wanted to be a little different or creative we might say, "I hope it will be nice to meet you", or, "time will tell if we enjoy one another." Being creative is exciting and stimulating. It is good for your mind, and it can keep improving one's life. So keep your life positive and stimulating, make your life fun to live and fun for others. Use your mind and your feelings to be creative as you wander through the day.

I am quite sure that there are many ways to be creative. Writing these chapters is certainly stimulating my thinking. So here we go. I'm going to turn myself loose and just write without censoring myself.

Perhaps that is a significant way to be creative. That is to give oneself the freedom to think without restrictions. So my first suggestion is that technique called brain storming. That's a technique I have allowed myself to do for the past few years. I wish my teachers and my professors had encouraged and stimulated me to brain storm.

So that I do not fail to communicate with you let me try to do my best to explain Brain Storming. Brain storming is a rather cute term. In my case it means a way to approach a situation, a problem, a goal and many other items. Let me try to provide a meaningful example. I just recently taught an exciting braille class in Ann Arbor, Michigan. Before one class I asked myself how might I do the class using my class plan and following it. For fun I wrote down any and all ideas that popped into my mind. By the way, that's the basic rule for brain storming. While you are brain storming do not limit your thinking. Just let your mind express any and every idea that pops up. So I asked myself the question:

After I have my class outlined how shall I follow that outline or plan? I'm going to let myself Brain Storm that right now. It is not the list I made a month ago. I'm just going to do it right now.

How shall I follow my class plans this week?

Write the outline in braille and follow it.
Write the outline in print and have a student direct me.
Put the outline in a recording and listen to that outline as I go.
Invite a child to class to control or guide me.
Have a friend on the phone and keep me on the right track.
Make an acronym to guide me through the class.
Just follow my thinking as I go and do not have any kind of plan.
Just record the outline ahead of time and play the recording as I go.
Do a video tape to present to the class.
Give a student an outline and let that student guide me through the class.
Take food to class and eat as I go with each piece of food representing one topic for the class.
Make little cards with each topic on a card.
Have the state governor join the class, and guide me with my outline.

There is a sample of a brain storming process in deciding how I would teach my class. You may be thinking that some of those ideas are unreasonable or not possible. That is quite true, but after the brain storming then it is time to look through the ideas, and evaluate what to do. Any of those ideas could lead to an interesting and a meaningful way to teach my class. My suggestion is that Brain storming is one good way to be creative, and it sure can be fun. Interestingly, having fun certainly stimulates one's creativity. I just read the above sentence, that sentence is strictly my opinion.

Before leaving this technique of brain storming perhaps I should say that there are different ways to brain storm. Here are a few:

1. Just brain storm by yourself.
2. Brain storm with a friend.
3. Brain storm with a group of people.
4. Brain storm with your husband or wife. I wish brain storming had been part of the forty-five and and half years that I was married to Laura. She would have been so good and stimulating at brain storming.

Remember when brain storming there is no censoring or evaluating of ideas. Any and every idea should be expressed. The evaluation comes after the brain storming session is over.

Some things we might try to keep our minds creative and interesting. I think the first objective is to keep our minds interesting to ourselves. Then to be interesting and stimulating to others.

When I was teaching I had the good fortune of teaching with an interesting friend and colleague. We encouraged one another to think freely and creatively. For instance, we took our students on a four day camp outing. One of the meals during this time was called our Backward Dinner. We all loved it. We started with dessert, then our main course, and after that we had our salad. Following that we did a camp song, and can you guess how we ended? Yes! your right! We said grace. The students really enjoyed the adventure as did the adults.

Since I am writing about living a creative life I will end this chapter by writing a poem. Poetry has meaning to me as you know. I like poetry because you can say a great deal enjoyably and in a few words. So, Ted, what should I write about? What about a quick poem about creativity?

First, I just had a thought. Every once in a while I will send an email to a friend that is poetic. Again, it helps me to keep my mind creative and thinking out of the box. But here's why I'm telling you this. So many times I get an email reply. The friend to whom I sent my email poetic message responds poetically. Of course, I really enjoy their poetic replies.

Now for my own mental stimulation here's just a quick poem hopefully of interest; it will be interesting for me!

Try To Be Creative

Why should we TRY to be creative?
We should erase try and just be innovative!
Let our minds soar out to the sky,
Let thoughts and ideas keep flowing by!

Try is a word to eliminate,
Just be creative and live real great,
Just be creative is my cry,
Let your mind flow high in the sky!

Summary

To quite an extent the above poem makes for a good chapter summary, but here is my chapter epilogue. I threw in the word epilogue to shock all of you including myself! Here's my short summary.

1. When being creative think out of the box.

2. Take a short time to brain storm either with yourself or do it with others. Maybe I'll encourage myself to do some brain storming with others.

Chapter joke:

Permit me to be bold and maybe a little creative.

Question: Walter why were you in jail?

Walter's reply: What do you mean? I have never been in jail!

Reply: Well! you told me you have a Cell phone. Isn't that where you get cell phones?

# Chapter 7

# We Are Curious

CURIOSITY

I am curious about myself and others,
I am interested in all my sisters and brothers,
My curiosity keeps me interested in this exciting life,
I am truly curious and interested in my wonderful wife!

I am curious about this fabulous earth,
I am interested in babies right from their birth!
I'm curious about everything relating to the sun,
Thinking about our earth is really fun!

Curiosity is now where you'll find my heart,
So now let's let this chapter start!

?????????-

This is an interesting topic to reflect upon and to write about.
Being curious about people, about things, about the earth, about
the sun, is a great way to live. I suggest that we should choose
consciously to be curious and interested. In fact, now that I am
thinking about curiosity, I would suggest that parents and
teachers make that part of their relationships with their
children and their students. How about going further with this
notion? Why not make curiosity a part of your relationship with
yourself?

Let me just ramble and reflect. Please remember that I am only
thinking and suggesting. I am not telling you what to think nor
what to do. I would like very much for you to follow your own
thinking and your own path.

Let me start by suggesting that we probably might be curious about ourselves. That is, evaluate and ask yourself questions about how you live. Be interested and curious about your daily actions, about how you choose to spend your time. I'm not suggesting that you criticize yourself but that you might want to be curious about and interested in your way of doing things.

I presently am going through a period in my life in which I am rather tired quite a bit. I have been asking myself about that. I have and am in the process of talking with my doctor to find out what could be going wrong. Yes, indeed! I want to get my energy back but I am also curious about what has happened in my life. The bottom line here is that maybe we should be curious and interested about all aspects of ourselves.

Next, I'd recommend that we be interested in other people. Talk positively and encouragingly to your family and your friends. I think that is one wonderful characteristic that all married couples could share and it could enrich their relationship. To be curious about and fascinated with your wife or husband could personally be so exciting. Moreover, it would elevate your partnership so much.

When it comes to our children, what could be more inspiring for the children than to have us interested in their lives. That's something I shall really get into right away. I will increase my interest, curiosity, and support in terms of my children and grandchildren.
Then there are other friends and strangers that we could express curiosity about.

There is so so much to stimulate our minds and keep us curious and involved. This earth, the sun, and the planets that make up our solar system is absolutely fascinating to me.

Let me cogitate about maybe just a few techniques for being curious.
I'm sure you can think of others.

1. Ask "what if" question. What if I cooked this meat loaf in water and peanut butter? What if I ate my main meal at breakfast instead of in the evening? What if I took a little time every day to exercise? What If questions can stimulate many interesting and exciting thoughts.

2. How does that work? How does the refrigerator keep food cool, what is the process in refrigeration? How far is the sun from our earth? How long does it take sunlight to travel from the sun to our earth? How far is it from where I live to the north and or south pole? How might we make our democracy work better and more efficiently? This could go on and on in different areas of life. But I'm sure you get the idea that I am expressing.

Interestingly, I just had a desire for a little to eat. I decided to make a little bowl of oatmeal. Then I got thinking about oatmeal. My thoughts were rather fun for me. First, I wondered where oat meal comes from? I answered myself by saying that I thought it was made from oats that are grown on a farm. Then, the next question I asked myself was what is the procedure for taking oats from the field and preparing it to be eatable by people like me. I am rather sure that it is not too complex, but perhaps I will pursue this just for interest and fun.

I wish that my teachers and parents had encouraged and promoted my curiosity when I was a boy. The one thing about me that my teachers and parents really did not completely grasp was that because I cannot see I needed to touch things to really learn about them. It is with great interest that I divert a little and tell you about how I learn about material objects. I have written a poem about how I learn. The main concept is that my fingers I use in place of having vision. In fact, let me meander a little and tell you an insightful experience I had back in 1954. The concept that I mentioned above namely, that I see with my fingers was really brought to my attention because of this experience.

When I was at Michigan State University, a truly positive girl read to me, and then we became friends started going out on dates. One afternoon I was in Jan's dormitory room with several other girls. Of course, I was interested in what she had in her room. I was "looking" no to be precise "touching" things on the top of her dresser. One of Jan's friends said something like: "Boy, Ted's hands are all over the place". Jan simply responded "that's because Ted sees with his fingers". That experience did and still does mean much to me. It brought to my attention the importance of my fingers because I had no vision to see things.

Over the years I have gotten into touching and learning. If I am not embarrassed about my blindness, then others are not. They encourage and help me to be curious about things and to feel and understand things.

Now I certainly have diverted my attention from the theme of this chapter. I hope my experiences and examples have stimulated our thinking-yours and mine.

Summary

Curiosity is a great characteristic to develop. I suggest that it is a good characteristic to develop in ourselves and to encourage in others. In other words, be interested in and curious about life.

Chapter Humor

Question: Why did the teacher tell her student that his grades were all under water?

Answer: Because they were all below c level!

# Chapter 8
# Develop a sense of humor

Take Time To Laugh

It struck my mind as I started to write this chapter that If we are addressing laughter and humor we should start the chapter with a bit of humor. So! let me start with what I still think is a humorous experience. This occurred in the year 1990. It will also give you a glimpse into the humor of my wonderful wife, Laura.

Back in February of 1990 Laura decided to attend a church conference in Ann Arbor, Michigan. The conference was a ladies conference. This conference was to be held at the end of March. So for at least a month I let all my friends know that Laura was going away for the weekend. I let it be known that I planned to have my house flowing with ladies all weekend long. I'm sure that I don't have to tell you this, but I was having fun joking about my weekend. I expected to spend a quiet two days looking forward to Laura's return.

I got off the bus on my way home from school that Friday afternoon. I think it was about 5:45. I walked about four blocks home and entered through the back door of our house. I anticipated a simple supper and a relaxed evening.

At about 6:15 my door bell rang. I answered the door. There were two lady friends of ours. By six thirty my living room was packed with ten ladies who were our friends. Laura set this all up based upon my telling how I could hardly wait for Laura's trip to Ann Arbor. That I planned to have lady after lady visit me all weekend. Unknowingly, Laura set this up that Friday evening.

My house was filled with our lady friends. I decided to order some pizza, and we had a vivacious 2.5 hours together. That gives you some insight into my spirited and humorous wife.

I'm telling you this humorous story 24 years later, so you know that it had to touch my heart. I could tell you many more joyful Laura stories, but this gets us off to a good start for this chapter; the theme being humor and laughter.

One of the magnificent qualities that God has provided to we human beings is the ability to laugh. It is a gift that we all, I suggest, should treasure and use daily. One of the joys of my career was the laughter that my colleague Margaret and I shared daily with our students. Margaret use to say "You can't get through a day with our youngsters without laughing several times". That was very true. We encouraged laughter and so did our students.

If I were to run a school, I believe that I would start each day with the national anthem and then with a joke. My purpose would be to start each day with laughter. In fact, Margaret and I joined our two elementary school classes starting each day. Besides an uplifting song we typically shared some humor with our students. Now, it was not just Margaret and I who shared humor. Our youngsters would also at times have a joke or funny experience to share. I remember when six year old Kyle would quite often come to school with a joke. Here's one of his jokes that I want to share with you.

My class and Margaret's class met each morning together. After the national anthem Kyle said "May I tell a joke"? We eagerly said go ahead. Here's Kyle's joke.

He said "What did the boy octopus say to the girl octopus?" Of course, we said "please tell us, Kyle". He said "the boy octopus said to the girl octopus: May I hold your hand, your hand, your hand, your hand, your hand, your hand, your hand, your hand!"

I am smiling as I read Kyle's joke and it brought to mind a funny joke that a Lincoln Park High girl told us when I was teaching at the high school. So here's another laugh.

Question: What did the girl rock say to the shy boy rock?

Answer: I wish you were a little boulder!
I have always enjoyed that one since about 2003.

I feel a desire to digress just a little. Margaret had a joyful sense of humor. She use to tell people that she was my daytime wife and Laura was my night time wife. Then she'd add, "Please don't mix us up!" I perhaps should add that it fills my heart with joy to tell you that Margaret and Laura became really good friends. That meant so much to me.

Develop A Sense Of Humor

The theme or topic of this chapter is that we should all keep laughter and humor in our lives. Take time daily to smile, to laugh, and to be humorous. If I were to go back to my wonderful teaching career, I think that I would include in my teaching strategy the principles of laughter. As you already know laughter was a part of our every day in school, but I think that I might have carried it just a little further.

Thus, I would teach the value of laughing and how healthy laughing is to us all. Then, we would cover the ways to implement laughter. Now, I want to explicitly mention this to you. I am strongly opposed to laughter that downgrades people. I know there are jokes out there about blonde ladies, about polish people, and about men and women. Any joke or comment that is meant to be humorous, but denigrates anyone, to me is not humorous and should not occur. I encourage only positive humor and joy, nothing negative or disparaging. That to me is mighty important.

Thus, I encourage you, and I encourage myself, to work at laughing and being humorous. As I write this, I strongly believe that as part of our education we should all be encouraged and taught how to laugh and be filled with joy in our hearts.

Now, after writing the above, I would encourage all of us to promote and enjoy the humor of others. Here I go again with my personal experiences. Many times people say or do something humorous, but someone will say something negative about what was said. For instance, I have a really good friend, and I told him something laughable and funny. He said something like this: "That is so terrible". I had meant to be humorous and joyful, but my first response was a hurt feeling. I basically overcame the down feeling knowing he was a good friend and that he really did find what I said joyful and humorous. However, I would say that rather than he saying something negative that was meant to be positive, why not say something like. "Hey! that was really funny, or I sure enjoyed your humor." I know it is common to respond with a negative comment when someone is humorous, but I would simply suggest that we all might and in fact, should, think and speak positively to one another.

Enjoy The Humor Of Others

That brings us to the humor of our friends and of others. I would recommend that we encourage one another to be humorous and to laugh. We should enjoy the humor of other people. Therefore, we should respond with smiles and laughter. We should make positive and supportive remarks about the humor that others share with us.

Wouldn't it be wonderful if we all would live with joy in our hearts. To repeat, smiling, laughing, being happy is a quality that God has provided for we human beings. Right from the start I would encourage each of us to use that ability to smile and laugh.

You know, just this minute it struck me that I wish that I could see people's smiles. That must be a marvelous ability that all of you with sight have. That is, to enjoy the smiles of your fellow humans. How thrilling and fulfilling it must be to look at another person and enjoy their smiles and their laughter. I sure enjoy the laughter of others. I think it would be a big bonus to see the faces of other people and to share their smiles.

Please do not think I am being negative because I cannot see. I am genuinely grateful for all the abilities God has given me. I dwell on what I have and not on on what I have not. However, I do admire how fantastic vision is for those who can see. I am grateful for all of you who can see. I was always so grateful for the fact that Laura could see. It enhanced both our lives. So enjoy everything you have and do not feel bad or dwell on what you do not have!

Before getting to the summary I just had a thought I'd like to share with you. many people when they are being friendly, warm, or humorous with me will gently tap on my shoulder when they are being funny. They convey a lot in a positive way to me.

Summary

Be sure to enjoy laughing and humor. Make being humorous in a positive manner part of your life. Keep humor positive not negative. Take time to enjoy the humor of your fellow humans. Incorporate laughter as an element of your day to day living.

I wonder, should I skip the end-of-chapter joke??

Chapter Humor

Because this chapter emphasizes humor, instead of a joke or riddle: I am going to share another personal and humorous story with all of you. So please enjoy this great episode!

Once per week my friends Tony and Ron get together with me for a joyful run. Actually we now don't really run. We in reality do a rapid walk and talk.

Recently they arrived in their car and said we would be going to a special running area. Strangely, they had me sit in the front seat. Normally Ron and tony would be in the front and I would sit in the back seat. But this day Ron was in the back and I sat in front with Tony, who was driving. No! they won't let me drive!! Perhaps, knowing them, I might have been suspicious. However, I didn't even think about or question why I was in the front.

We drove to the woodsy area where we would run.

We use a thin rope about twelve inches long to run together. I hold one end and the person, Ron in this case, held the other end.

We started running and talking. All of a sudden a strange thing happened. Ron's voice had changed from being a man to being a lady. What a surprise that was!

Ron's daughter Ashley was with us and she was quietly in the back seat. That's why I was put in front. We started our run and quietly and unknown to me Ron surreptitiously gave his end of the rope to his daughter Ashley. All of a sudden in total surprise I was running with his daughter. It was so funny and so joyful.

# Chapter 9

# Be Kind To Yourself And To Others

MY PLEDGE TODAY

Be Kind

Let me keep this pledge in mind,
Today to myself I shall be kind!
Kindness to myself is where I must start,
This kindness should come from deep in my heart!

If to myself I will be loving and kind,
Then what do you think that I surely will find?
So kindly I'll be to my sisters and brothers,
Kindness will be an easy expression to others!

?????????-

The word kind is a simple four letter word. Yet it means so much in terms of a person relating to himself and relating to other people. I will start with a little thought about being kind to oneself. I believe that that is where kindness should begin.

As I think about this inspiring and exciting concept, I ask myself what in the world am I talking about. What is or does it mean to be kind? I guess I would have to say that kindness starts out with respecting and encouraging oneself. What I am saying is that we should have uplifting and positive thoughts and feelings about who we are. WE should really like ourselves and we should have great respect for who we are. I seriously encourage parents and teachers to have respect for their children and students. Moreover, we should teach children and teach each other to be kind and caring to ourselves. Kindness like joy, happiness, confidence, and so forth is what we should be every moment of the day to ourselves, as we go through each day of our lives.

I think there should be a class in school teaching these chapters. What an outstanding and important class it would be to teach a class called PIP. I sure would have found such a class so valuable and so important when I was a boy. I would love to have had such an experience. I have no doubt at all that it would have been by far my most important class ever.

So now we are being kind to ourselves. That I believe will lead us to being kind to others. Each of us should keep kindness in mind. We should watch our words, our behavior, our attitudes with the idea of being kind. That is, kind to oneself and kind to others. We should watch our actions and our words to make sure that they are supportive, encouraging, and kindly.

Perhaps I might ask myself what might be some of the characteristics of being kind. First, think and say positive things about oneself and about others. Do not say negative and defeating comments about yourself or about others. See yourself and others as being competent, capable, and able. Monitor unkind and negative acts and words about yourself and about your fellow human beings. How exciting would life be if we could focus on the positive and fulfilling aspects of living.

I might suggest that we monitor our actions and our words as we go through the day. We could think about what we do and what we say. Our criteria for what we do and say would be "am I kind". Am I kind to myself; am I kind to others? We might even carry this notion one step further. We might think about being kind to this earth that God has provided for us. Are we treating ourselves, each other, and this excellent earth in a kindly manner?

As I reflect upon kindness, I ask myself how can I be kindly? Well, first, my thoughts and my words should be kind. Second, my actions should be kind. I should help myself and help others to live a happy and successful life on this potentially perfect planet. When I say Potentially, perfect, planet I am being quite poetic and dreaming. My dream is to have this earth where we live to be as perfect as possible. That's a goal and a dream. But again it is a positive one. And I guess that although this chapter is aimed at being kind to oneself and to others kindness will lead to happiness, achievement, and joy. I think that kindness to ourselves and others will help us to be lively and happy.

I realize that this is a short chapter, but I think it covers the topic adequately, so off I go to a brief summary.

Summary

As we go through each and every day, We should be kind to ourselves. As we go through each and every day, we should be kind to others. Being kind to oneself leads to be being kind to others. In fact, if we are not kind to ourselves, we probably would not be kind to others.

Chapter Riddle:

What should be the fourth word in this series?
Ant, Bird, horse,

Here's your choices:

dog, rabbit, elephant.

Answer: the next word is rabbit. Ant has three letters, bird has four letters, horse has five letters, so you want the next word to have six letters. That, of course, is rabbit.

# Chapter 10

# Be Adventurous And Courageous

ADVENTURE

LIFE should be an adventure for all,
If our life is an adventure, we'll have a ball!
Think of each moment as an exciting trip,
Sail through life like your on a ship!

In a real sense this chapter is encouraging me to do something adventurous. No! I am doing something adventurous. That's because I am not sure what to say in this chapter. So I just decided to go ahead and get started and make this chapter an adventure.

If we view life as an adventure, then certainly we can be having fun with our living. Adventures can be small or big. Small or big they can be mentally and physically stimulating. So whether we explore a store that we've never been in before, or whether we take a vacation cruise, we can perceive these things as adventures. Of course, every adventure should be exciting, fun, and stimulating. So give me permission to just give some examples of what I am writing about.

I just read the above paragraph and it stimulated me to include this paragraph. I would recommend to you and to myself, especially to myself, that we make every moment an adventure. Wouldn't that make life so exhilarating to keep every activity an adventure. Thanks for the insight. I shall start doing that. Additionally, in the above paragraph I mention that we have adventures big and small. As I read what I said, it struck me that we perhaps should not categorize our adventures as some big and some small. Each experience might be viewed as an outstanding adventure. Maybe we need not think in terms of big and small?

What is upcoming is for me something that I do to be courageous and adventurous. Please be cognizant that what is courageous and adventurous for me may not be so for you. The idea here is that I want to provide a few examples of adventuring for me. Hopefully they will stimulate you to decide upon adventures that are appropriate and meaningful for you.

First, when I am in an audience and the speaker or presenter says "are their any questions"? In the past I was afraid to ask a question. Nowadays, if I have a question I raise my hand and I ask the question. Back in past times I often, usually, did not ask questions. I thought that everyone else probably knew the answer and that I should just be quiet. First of all, if I have a question no matter if everyone else could answer it, I should still ask it. In addition, I have found that many times I ask a question and many people in the audience are glad I asked. It's a question that many would like the answer to.

Second, Sometimes I have a telephone call that I need to or should make. Quite often I am uncomfortable about making that particular call. I find that I might avoid or postpone making the call. I now encourage myself to make the call. Moreover, I think about the call in a positive manner. I tell myself that this is going to be fun and interesting. That all goes with the notion of enjoying every moment.

Third, just for the fun of it I go to a web site that I think might be interesting, valuable, and fun. I look at a new web site as an adventure, and therefore, loaded with fun.

There's three specific adventures that I personally find stimulating. Let me site, say, three more that are general and do not necessarily apply to me or to you.

Here's one that I'm tempted to say applies to young people, but as I think about it, it does not apply just to youngsters. The example is to ask a person a boy or a girl, man or woman, for a date or a meeting. That could be the adventure of having lunch together, meeting for a talk and coffee, going for a walk, and anything that would be an adventure for you or me.

The following example seems so simple, yet it could be a pleasant adventure. Go to a store that you don't usually explore. That could be a grocery store, office equipment store, clothing store, or any kind of store. It could be fun to do, and maybe we'd find a store of value that we had not experienced before. Again, do it just for the fun of an adventure.

Thirdly, take a trip, long or short, and do it with a spirit of adventure in your heart. My wife, Laura, had a great sense of adventure. She was interested in many many things. LAURA stimulated that sense of exploring and trying things just for the joy involved. She was such a positive influence in my life.

Summary

Be adventurous as you go through life. Enjoy each experience, and do not hesittate to do new things. Spend your time enjoying living, being positive, and having the sense that life is an adventure in your heart.

Chapter Humor:

Question: Why were the early days of history called the dark ages?

Answer: Because there were so many knights!

# Chapter 11

# Dreaming And goal Setting

DREAM

My advice to myself and maybe you'll agree?
Is to DIE daily; it'll set us free!
It's a three letter word, the first letter is D.
The D stands for dream. Please listen to me.

Take time to dream every single day,
That's so important, that's what I say!
So take time to dream, it will enrich your life,
Let your mind soar, take time out from strife,

Take time each day to put your head in a cloud,
Of this time you can surely be proud,
Dream away and don't delay,
This should be part of our every day!

?????????-

Perhaps the poem that I have chosen to introduce this chapter may have shocked or surprised you. The part of the poem to which I refer is the statement:

"My advice to myself and maybe you'll agree,
Is to DIE daily; it'll set you free!"

The word DIE in DIE Daily is an acronym. The acronym means to do the following daily:

Dream, Improve, Enjoy.

Thus, the idea therein is that we should Dream, we should keep Improving, and we should Enjoy living. Since the aim of this chapter is the notion that we should Dream and set goals, and enjoy pursuing those goals I won't delve into the Improve and Enjoy aspects of the poem. However, Chapter two is dedicated to enjoying one's life, and chapter twelve explores the idea of improving.

The further I get into the writing of this book, the more convinced I am becoming that schools should have a class for students called PIP. PIP would be a class where each student would get to know themselves and take time to Dream, To Improve, and to Enjoy their life. If I had had these insights 50 years ago, I would have somehow worked PIP into my teaching. I am sure to some extent I did that, but I would have made it a definite part of my teaching.

I have a friend who is a third grade teacher. One afternoon he told me that several of his students told him they wanted to be professional hockey players. He told me how he told them to forget such a wild idea. He told them that their chances of becoming a professional hockey player was almost impossible. My outlook on things like this is that that is uplifting and positively motivating to have a dream like this. Whether it would come true or not, it would lead you to enjoy hockey and to do your best. In other words, it is great to reach for the stars.

In Shad Helstetter's outstanding book called, "What to say when you talk to yourself," his first chapter deals, for me, with a thrilling way to live, that is to reach for the stars instead of keeping your feet on the ground. If anyone reading this book wants some inspiration, I sure highly recommend Shad's inspiring book.

As I wrote this, I paused just a moment to think how I wish when I was twelve years old I had a book like Shad's. It might have made a big impact on my life. Actually, Shad's book has been a significant influence in my life. Shad has encouraged me to keep dreaming and improving. By the way, Shad also made a significant difference in Laura's life.

As I write this chapter, I think how I wish I had talked more with my daughters about Dreaming, Improving, and Enjoying.

Let me get back to the theme of this chapter. That theme being to dream and to decide what dreams you would like to pursue and perhaps achieve. If you decide to pursue a particular dream, then, I suppose we can say that that dream has become a goal. If a dream is a goal, then a step in the direction of achieving your dream, now your goal, would be to establish a plan as to how you might accomplish your dream which is now your goal. Perhaps you'll let me give one rather simple example of one goal that I did surprise myself by setting and achieving.

On March 18, 1981, my daughter, Marla, asked me to go to the bank with her. She was 14 and had a check to cash. She thought she should have me their so they would cash her check. I told her the bank would be closing in five minutes, so we'd better run there instead of walk. We ran about 50 feet. I was so unfit that that was as far as I could run. I told Marla that we had to stop; I could not run further. We did make it to the bank, but I became fully aware of my poor physical condition.

It was then that I decided to start running and get into physical shape. Had someone told me that three years later, 1984, I would run a marathon, I would have thought that was a preposterous notion. I'd never ever be able to run 26.2 miles. I'd enjoy telling you the story of the trail that led to my marathon in 1984, but I'll just say that my 50 foot run with Marla began a whole new unexpected adventure in my interesting life. My personal view is that God started me on that adventure on March 18, 1981. I have thanked God many times for that experience.

It is interesting and shocking to me to reflect upon my youth. Never did a teacher or a counselor ever propose the idea of dreaming or goal setting. The more I think and write about these ideas the more I feel convinced that part of education should be a class called PIP. That is a class encouraging Personal Improvement. What a thrilling way to live one's life always trying to DIE DAILY. Again, DIE means to Dream, Improve, and Enjoy living here on this excellent earth.

Before concluding this chapter I will just include this notion. If possible, relate to positive people who will encourage you to believe in yourself, and support you in going after your dreams and your goals. Internal guidance and motivation are fundamental, but it helps to have support from others, too. Actually, if you are positive and optimistic with your feelings, thinking, and dreams I think that you will quite likely attract people who share your positive outlook. Thus, they will encourage you, and you will encourage them.

Summary

If we are motivated to keep improving, then dreaming should be part of our life. It is good to dream about one's life, and what one would like to achieve. Then the next step perhaps might be to evaluate your dreams and decide which one or which ones you really want to pursue.

Next comes turning dreams that you want to achieve into goals. Set goals short and long term and enjoy working toward those goals. Two important words in the above statement. First, Enjoy your efforts at moving forward toward your goals and dreams. The second word, is Working. Here the word working is positive. Make it fun going toward your goals. The word working is meant to be a positive and motivating word. Perhaps instead of saying working tward your goals I should change the word Working to Playing. Thus, enjoy Playing tward your goals. In fact, when I teach, I do not give homework. I give Home Play. Recently I had the joy of teaching a class in braille to some people in Ann

Arbor, Michigan. To conclude each class I would give them their Homeplay. At the end of class 6 I casually said, "Now here's your home work for the week". One of the lively ladies in the class quickly interrupted. She corrected me and said that she thought I gave Homeplay not Homework. I smiled joyfuly then, and am doing so right now. Thanks for correcting me Deborah.

Chapter Humor

Question: What time does a duck wake up?

Answer: At the quack of dawn!

# Chapter 12

# Growing and Improving

IMPROVE

As long as one is still alive,
Improvement is something for which to strive,
A person 'til death should always be growing,
The garden of life is meant for hoeing!

Live your life in a positive grove,
Keep it exciting with your every move,
Always keep striving to improve.

?????????-

I am sitting here thinking about this chapter. There are questions that I am asking myself. First off I believe we should be happy and peaceful about our current status in our life. So the idea of improving is an exciting and positive notion. It definitely is not negative!!

The idea in this chapter should be combined with the ideas in earlier chapters. Particularly the chapter on Enjoying Every Moment, and being Self-confident. Then the process of learning, growing, and improving can be just plain fun and delightful.

For example, a five year old youngster will probably be starting kindergarten. She or he will have the joy and fun of learning the alphabet. The joy of learning to read and write and get into adding and subtracting. The kindergarten adventure should be filled with fun and exciting for every child.

Jumping forward to high school and college a student should have the same experience. That is continuing to learn and grow with exuberance and enthusiasm. Every class should be loaded with inspiration and it should be joyful to be part of as a student. In my opinion, this should be a path that we choose to take all through our lives. As adults and as senior citizens we should be on the road of learning, growing, and Improving.

I note that I keep using the word Growing in this chapter. Let me be clear about the word growing in this situation. I am talking about growing in every aspect of life. That is, growing emotionally, intellectually, physically, learning new and interesting aspects of life.

This example just came to mind. My father-in-law, his name was Will, retired around age seventy. I'm not sure how this happened, but he began to play golf. Had I told him when he became 60 that he'd be playing and enjoying golf in ten years, he'd have laughed at such an idea. Somehow at about age 70 he got into golfing. He just plain enjoyed the challenge and the sport. He added this adventure to his already fascinating life.

I met and became friends with Will when he was sixty years old. Neither of us would have thought that ten years later we'd be playing golf together. Laura's dad was basically committed to farming. That was his life. However, ten years later he was still learning and growing.

The theme of this chapter is that I am recommending, by no means telling any of you, that perhaps life can be kept stimulating and fulfilling by keeping on growing and learning.

In fact, my friend and running partner, Nina, just read me an article from the newspaper about an eighty-seven year old lady who just graduated from college.

My thought here is that it keeps life positive, fulfilling, and enjoyable to keep learning new things and making your life happier and more adventurous. Certainly this is in synch with the preceding chapters, especially, chapter 2 where the theme is to Enjoy Each Moment, and the chapters about Creativity and Curiosity. Really the foundation of this chapter is based on all the preceding chapters.

Now, I shall do my best to follow my own advice. And once again, what I say to you is only for your thinking. Whatever you do, and above everything else, please, please, think for yourself. Guide and direct your own life internally, do not, do not, let others tell you what to do or control you in any way.

If you've read with understanding the above paragraphs, then I can tell you one thing I do in terms of helping myself to keep improving. I tell you this cautiously, for I'm not in any way recommending that this is what you should do. That is, of course, unless you would like to do it.

I retired a few years ago and after retirement, I started keeping a daily journal. I have found that to be stimulating and interesting. I'd like to say that I wish I had done this throughout my life, but I'm not sure that I would have taken the time to do so. As I write this, I am thinking that I wish I had spent a little time each day writing and reflecting. At one time during my teaching career I had my students at the end of the day write short journals about some of the things they did during the day. My purpose at the time was to get them to practice their writing skills. Then every Friday instead of journaling we each chose one day to share. I think that it was helpful to my super students to write and to think. Upon reflection, were I still to be teaching I am quite sure that I might get my students into journaling consistently.

Let me remind myself that this chapter has to do with growing and improving. For me, not necessarily for anyone else, journaling I believe helps me to keep improving. By journaling I think about what I did and how I did things. For me that is helpful. I'll just comment that for me journaling does seem to help me reflect upon my life, what I do, and how I do things. That, for me, can lead to growing and improving. That's for me not necessarily for you. You as I've said many times in this book, should do your own thinking and follow your own life pathway.

Summary

One way to keep life interesting and exciting might be to keep growing and improving. That's my recommendation. I have personally found that to be a positive and meaningful way to live here on earth.

Chapter humor:

Question: What did the judge say when the skunk entered the courq room?

Answer: Odor in the court!

# Chapter 13

# We should be aware of our assumptions

MAKING ASSUMPTIONS

Making assumptions can really be fun.
We assume that tomorrow we'll see the sun.
We make assumptions both day and night,
Much of the time we are probably right!

There's one area of our assumptions that we should drop,
Assuming what others are thinking and feeling we should stop.
We cannot know what's in another's mind,
Just remaining neutral is best you will find!

Your friend Sally passes you on the street,
With nary a word does she even greet.
She doesn't even give you the time of day,
She walks right by and looks the other way!

You assume that she's really mad at you,
So Sally, in the future, you will surely eschew!
You assume that she is mean, nasty, or unkind,
Maybe a better friend you should seek to find!

Why not think, "Sally did not speak as I went by,
That makes me curious and I wonder why."
Maybe Sally's mind is in some other place,
It's very possible she didn't even see my face.

In the restaurant, there sat Frank,
He didn't speak - what a crank!
Maybe his thoughts were on a letter he had to write,
He was engrossed in what to say upon getting home that night.

I've called jan twice without a reply,
I assume she doesn't like me, is my sigh,
Later you find that Jan was really sick,
You jumped to a conclusion much too quick!

Assuming what others think and feel
Is living in a world that is not very real.
Here's a happier, healthier way to live,
Avoid assumptions that are not affirmative.

??????????

Here we go into an important area of each of our lives. In all honesty, I am delving into a topic that I have not really explored in the past. However, upon thinking about this subject, I believe it to be really important and one that I sure wish I'd been introduced to when I was a youngster. Help me if you will to get my thinking started about assumptions.

I will begin by mentioning several simple assumptions to get our thinking on to the assumption subject.

Here's my first example: It is just after twelve noon. I shall assume that by ten o'clock tonight I will be tired and ready to sleep. That's a reasonable, easy, and probably accurate assumption. It may be correct, however this assumption could be inaccurate come ten o'clock. This may depend upon what I do in the afternoon. My point being that it is an assumption. It is nothing serious.

How about one more simple but not serious assumption? Let's say that it is Saturday. I work Mondays through Fridays. I assume that I will go to work this coming Monday. During my working years I assumed that to be true every Saturday. Now let's just say that on Sunday I awoke not feeling well; I had come down with the flu. Thus, my assumption on Saturday that I would work on Monday has turned out not to be true. Thus, my Saturday assumption was incorrect.

I hope that I have in a real simple way given a couple of clear ideas about what assumptions are. Further, that many of our assumptions are correct. Moreover, when what we assume to be trrue does not happen, we comfortably adjust to the situation.

One more simple personal example. I am right now assuming that I will be golfing on Wednesday morning. That's a good assumption for me, it will occur depending upon other circumstances in my life, and, of course, what the weather happens to be Wednesday on this fascinating planet upon which I reside.

This is going to challenge my mind. I know that it is so important, and therefore it is good for me not delve into the thinking about making negative assumptions that hurt and limit oneself, and that get in the way of healthy, happy, and joyous friendships.

I will try to site some examples of making assumptions that can get in the way of good relationships and blemish promoting happiness.

I will start with the this example. This I referred to earlier in the book. I use to be down right afraid to ask questions in meetings and in classes. My Assumptions were that they were questions that would sound stupid and make me look bad to others. I therefore did not confidently and comfortably be fully part of classes and meetings. In fact, as I write this to you and me, I find that that is true even in one-to-one relationships. I am working at being more interesting in my conversations and in participating in meetings and classes.

Now, I am not saying that I will argue and dispute with people. I am saying I will clarify what we are discussing. I will try to understand what I do not understand. I want the freedom and peace of talking and discussing things with individuals and in meetings and in groups.

At present I am on the Resident Advisory Council here at Henry Ford Village. I try to understand the topics being discussed. If I do not understand, I calmly ask for clarification and understanding. Wait, I'm off track somewhat. I watch my thinking, and I watch my assumptions so that I do not assume the wrong thing. Now can I give at least one meaningful example, because this is really important.

This morning my grandson, Dave, who is staying with me this summer, left for work without saying good-bye. My first assumption was that he was not being very friendly. Then, I went a step further and thought, his mind must have been focused on something like getting to work on time, or, perhaps he was tired and not thinking about saying good-bye. Finally, my thought was that I need not make any assumptions at all. How would I know what he was thinking. If it was important, I could ask him, allowing him to tell me what he was thinking. That way I did not make any false assumptions.

Having said the above, there are two things that I might recommend. First, do not assume you know what another person is thinking. Second, if you need to know or want to know what someone is thinking simply ask them.

This chapter has been important for me. It has made me think about my own thinking and hopefully will help me to avoid any assumptions. I just said any assumptions; but I shall somewhat change that notion. If we choose to make assumptions about what 'others are thinking, make those assumptions positive and not negative. Living positively is really so powerful. It provides happiness, and leads to good relationships amongst people.

Summary

First we make assumptions constantly. That is, we assume our car will start tomorrow morning. What we need to watch and monitor is not thinking we know what others are thinking. We probably should not assume we know what another person has in mind. If we want or need to know, simply ask them. I shall be thinking further about this topic. I will also either not make any assumption about what another person has in mind, or if I do I will be fully aware that I am only assuming what someone else is thinking.

Chapter humor:

Question: Why was Santa's little helper depressed?
Answer: Because he had low elf esteem.

# Chapter 14
# Life With God

God is Here

God is always always here,
God is so loving and so dear,
With God I need not live in fear!
I can live with joy and with cheer!

God is with me all the time,
It makes my life so sublime,
Each moment I live without any fear,
That's because God is always here!

God is constantly in my mind,
He treats me oh so very kind!
Thank You God for my life so pleasant,
That's because you're always present!

?????????-

This will do it! This is my final chapter in PIP. IN this
chapter I will be honest, and I will share with whoever decides
to read this chapter the route that I have followed in my life
that has led me to God. It has been a complex route, and I am so
grateful that God has been there for me and with me. Please do
not read what follows and think that I am being critical or
unkind to how others have influenced me. I hope to be honest and
to be kind.

With great gratitude and happy heart I shall start by saying
that God never abandoned me. God was always present even when I

did not know that. I am so grateful to God and his guidance throughout my life.

I just turned on my BrailleNote, and I read the poem that begins this chapter. I wish that I had always lived and believed the poem above called "God is here". I keep this wonderful notion in mind almost all the time.

I am perplexed as to what to say in this important chapter. Much of my life has been a struggle getting connected with God and, if I can say, following God's guidance.

After writing the above sentence I must digress again. I referred to God as HIM. We tend to think of God as being a man. I personally believe in God as God. I do not picture God as being male or female. My concept here is that I do not, think of God as Him, or Father nor as Her or Mother. I think of God as God. Forgive me if I offend anyone with this paragraph. The nice part is that it has made or given me the opportunity to think about God.

Let me get back to the purpose and aim of this chapter. Please know that I am not in any way trying to tell you what to believe or how to believe in God. I'm just in this chapter allowing myself to tell you about the bumpy road I have followed in getting to personally be guided by God. You in no way, should think that I am telling you what to think or if you and God should be buddies. Hey! there's a good word for me. That's because I think of God as my friend, my guide, my buddy. He has led me all of my life. What's so fabulous about that is that Much of my life I did not know that God was guiding me. I thank God for His constant guidance throughout my life.

Well, I just read the above part of this chapter, and I believe that I have said what I want to say. So I shall conclude this chapter and therefore this book. It has been exciting and enjoyable to write. And! I shall end by saying thank You to God for helping me to write this book, and for guiding me, on this important adventure.

## Summary

It is with joy that I have finally become connected to or related with God. It has been quite a journey, and I am grateful that God has been with me, often unknowingly by me, throughout my life. I shall also end this chapter with some humor. At first a thought passed through my mind that because this chapter is spiritual in nature I should not include any humor. Then, I quickly realized that that's one glorious quality that God has provided all of us. Namely, the ability to laugh.

Question: What did Adam say to his wife on Christmas day?

Answer: Well! it's Christmas, Eve!